T0113540

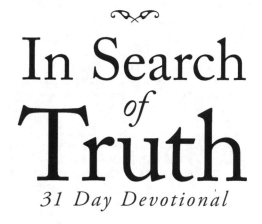

In Search
of
Truth

31 Day Devotional

DeLinda N. Baker

WESTBOW
PRESS®
A DIVISION OF THOMAS NELSON
& ZONDERVAN

This book is a work of non-fiction. Unless otherwise noted, the author and the publisher make no explicit guarantees as to the accuracy of the information contained in this book and in some cases, names of people and places have been altered to protect their privacy.

WestBow Press books may be ordered through booksellers or by contacting:

WestBow Press
A Division of Thomas Nelson & Zondervan
1663 Liberty Drive
Bloomington, IN 47403
www.westbowpress.com
1 (866) 928-1240

ISBN: 978-1-9736-0826-4 (sc)
ISBN: 978-1-9736-0825-7 (e)

Print information available on the last page.

WestBow Press rev. date: 11/28/2017

Table of Contents

Introduction

There is a surge of fake news overtaking media outlets in the 21st century. Fake news is the intentional misrepresentation, exaggeration or distortion of the facts in the hopes of swaying viewpoints and confusing its audience.

Fake news stands in stark contrast to the unbiased objective truth. Integrity and truth become secondary to the desire to sensationalize and sway opinions. The belief the "end justifies the means" places the interests of the few, whatever their motivation, as more important than the truth. To some, the moral obligation to report truth versus fiction is no longer straightforward or clear.

The question as to what is truth has been discussed for centuries by philosophers and various religions. Is truth divine and absolute? Does truth change relative to the beliefs and customs of various cultures evolving over time? There is a plethora of different answers and viewpoints offered on this topic. It is easy to see why people are confused as we seek to find truth around us, particularly in our politicians, government, and core beliefs. So, who should we trust to guide us in this important quest?

There is only one being who knows man inside out, discerns the plans of leaders and completely understands all that has been created. That being is God. So, it makes sense that we look to the book which teaches us about God, the Bible, to find truth. The Bible teaches that truth is absolute and does not change with time or culture. One of the defining characteristics of God is truth. God never lies to us. He does not distort the facts or seek to manipulate us. In love, he always tells us the absolute truth. Further, the precepts and commands of God teach us how to become agents of truth ourselves and to discern truth and deception in others.

Join us for a daily devotional as we explore scriptures that discuss truth. My hope is that each of us will become more discerning in recognizing truth in what we are told, in our culture and in ourselves.

"Where I found truth, there found I my God, who is the truth itself." – Saint Augustine, <u>The City of God</u>

I

A God of Truth

One of the defining characteristics of God is truth. Every aspect of God is true and trustworthy. God the Father, Son and Holy Spirit are all described as true. The inspired Word of God, like its source, is reliable and true. God's precepts and commands are trustworthy and everlasting.

God is the origin of truth. Unless we begin with this fundamental understanding, it will be impossible to find and know truth.

There are many false gods worshipped by mankind. If people follow false creeds, they will quickly find themselves on the path to lies, deception, and an inability to discern and know real truth. In Romans 1:21, Paul talks about the fate of individuals who rejected God—"their thinking became futile and their foolish hearts were darkened".

To start on the journey of truth, one must first begin with God. One must recognize His absolute authority to dictate truth to mankind.

Day 1

God is True

But the LORD is the true God;
he is the living God, the eternal
King. —Jeremiah 10:10a

Where does truth originate from? To recognize truth, there must be an absolute, unwavering, and moral standard from which everything else is compared. In Jeremiah 10:10, we learn four important facets of the true God.

First, the Lord is the "true God". The Bible teaches that there are many false Gods, but there is only one true God, the God of Abraham, Isaac, and Jacob. All other gods are men's imaginations or forged by their hands; they are not alive. Imputing life or conscience to false gods is futile, leading to emptiness and loss.

Second, God is Truth. Truth is not something God is seeking. God is the essence, the source and the very definition and standard of truth. Without God as a standard for comparison, it would be impossible to know what is authentic.

Third, God is living. Truth is vital, just and constant. It emanates from its source, God, and reveals itself through word, actions, and thoughts.

Finally, truth is everlasting. God is immutable,

which means he never changes, either in character or in purpose. Because of this, we can know that truth emanating from God is also constant and unchanging. Those qualities that are true, right, just, good, and pure never change. They may be packaged in different times, events or personalities, but their underlying nature remains the same.

So, how do we as Christians recognize truth? The Bible says to love God with all your heart, soul, mind, and strength (Mark 12:30). In loving God fully and searching the scriptures, we will find what truth looks like and know the standard by which all facts, events, and actions should be measured.

PRAYER: Heavenly Father, we acknowledge that you are the one TRUE God. You are alive and characterized by everlasting truth. Reveal to us your true nature as we draw near to you. Guide us in our understanding of truth. Amen.

Day 2

Jesus is True

Jesus answered, "I am the way and
the truth and the life." —John 14:6a

Just as God the Father is described as "true", His Son is also characterized as being "true". The Webster dictionary describes the behavior of truth as "sincerity in action, character, and utterance". The essence of truth is defined as "the body of real things, events, and facts"[1]. While in the dictionary, the body refers to a grouping of items comprising a whole, I look at this definition and see truth embodied in one individual's body—that of Jesus.

Jesus is a perfect reflection of his true Father. In John 15:1, he describes himself as the "true vine". Jesus being true is fundamental to knowing that our core Christian beliefs can be trusted. For example, Jesus claimed to be God, he asked us to follow and obey his many teachings on righteous living, and he has said that he will return some day to judge all men. If Jesus was a liar, manipulator, or crazy, would you place your eternal future in his hands? Of course not.

Jesus embodies truth and nurtures truth in those who follow him. When I was in college, I often went out drinking with my friends. However, as I grew in my faith, I began to feel less comfortable with participating in an activity that clouded my judgment. I began to understand life as Jesus sees it—the way it really was. Real friends. Real decisions. Real consequences. Real feelings. Real caring for others. Real truth. Suddenly, drinking and pretense at life lost its attraction.

Consider today how you reflect your Lord by being grounded in truth. Just as Jesus reflects his Father, you are to reflect Jesus in your life.

PRAYER: Thank you Father for giving us your Son. How blessed we are that he has come and died for our sins. Just as the Father is characterized by truth, his Son Jesus is also the way, the truth and the life. Help us today to reflect truth in our character and actions so that we, as children of God, may reflect your standards in righteousness. Amen.

Day 3

God's Word is Right and True

For the word of the Lord is right and true; he
is faithful in all he does. —Psalm 33:4

Not only is God himself described as true, but everything he speaks is true and right. The outpouring of his true word is seen in his constant, reliable, and consistent actions. As it says in Proverbs 33:4, he is "faithful" in all he does.

Not long ago, a well-known newscaster was fired from a cable news channel. He had lied about a story that had occurred oversees and embellished the facts to make the story more sensational and make himself look more heroic. The news station knew that if people could not believe the news he offered each night, then soon they would stop watching. His reputation and trustworthiness had been tarnished.

John F. Kennedy once quipped, ". . . we must never forget that the highest appreciation is not to utter words, but to live by them."[2] People instinctively desire to hear the truth. They want to know that the decisions they make are based on reliable information. Therefore, it is of paramount importance that God speaks the truth. Proverbs 8:6-8 reassures us, "Listen, for I [wisdom] have trustworthy things to say; I open my lips to speak what is right. My mouth speaks what is true, for my lips detest wickedness. All the words of my mouth are just; none of them is crooked or perverse."

Consider two synonyms of truth, trustworthy and just. If an individual is speaking the truth, then you can trust that what he says is worthy. If an individual is established in truth, his actions and decisions will be just and fair. Ask yourself today—can people rely on what you say as truthful? What do your words say about your character?

PRAYER: Lord, your Word is right and true. There is nothing that compares to the reliability and faithfulness of your Word. We can fully depend on it! Teach us your Word, Lord. Help us to discipline our minds to study and understand its truth. Amen.

Day 4

God's True Laws are Everlasting

> Your righteousness is everlasting and your
> law is true. . . Yet you are near, Lord,
> and all your commands are true. Long
> ago I learned from your statutes that you
> established them to last forever. . . All your
> words are true; all your righteous laws are
> eternal. —Psalm 119:142, 151-152, 160

Everything God speaks is true, righteous, and everlasting. So, if follows logically, that the laws and commands that God gives mankind to live by are also true, righteous and everlasting.

To say that something is true is to say it is factual and accurate. To say that it is righteous is to say it is morally pure and virtuous. To say that it is everlasting is to say it is eternal. Literally, God's laws and commands never stop being true and righteous. The laws and commands of the Bible have been true in the past, are still true and applicable today, and will be true for perpetuity.

So, where do we find God's commands by which we live? Many of them are found in Exodus and Deuteronomy, as God laid out guidelines for the new nation of Israel. Other commands are found throughout the Old Testament, including the Psalms and Proverbs. But if you are looking for the cliff-note version, Jesus summarized all of the commands in one word—Love. In Matthew 22:37-40, Jesus said that all the law and Prophets hung on two commandments—"Love the Lord your God with all your heart . . . soul and . . . mind" and "love your neighbor as yourself". Without love, the heart of truth is skewed and becomes distorted.

Has anyone ever told you that God's laws are old-fashioned and no longer relevant? This couldn't be further from the truth. God's laws are timeless and culminate in love. Loving God and others is never irrelevant. Consider today how God's laws and precepts are timeless and everlasting.

PRAYER: Lord, your decrees are more precious than gold and sweeter than the honeycomb (Psalm 19:10). We meditate on them night and day (Psalm 1:2). As we seek to obey your precious and loving commands, transform us into the men and women you desire us to be. Amen.

Day 5

God's Laws are Trustworthy

The law of the Lord is perfect,
refreshing the soul. The statutes of the
Lord are trustworthy, making wise
the simple. —Psalm 33:4

Since all of God's laws and commands are true, they are perfect and trustworthy as well. This means we can have absolute confidence that following them will be good for us. In the Bible, we find laws which establish boundaries of behavior, precepts which provide guidelines and rules, and commands which direct our actions. The important thing to remember is that all of them are intended to lead us to live holy godly lives.

If we live by these principles, not only are we pleasing God but the Bible tells us that God's laws will make us wise (Psalm 19:7). At the very least, following them will make us right. And we will be living in full harmony with creation, which was ordered by a true, orderly and perfect God.

Knowing God's laws and commands requires an investment on each individual's part. Unfortunately, you can't learn them by good intentions or osmosis. You have to read, study and apply these principles to your life in order to learn them. Until we learn what is true, we will have difficulty identifying those things that are false.

When we search for truth in the world, we should measure it against the high standards of behavior that God has taught us in his Word. If a story, event, or even a person's testimony fails to meet these standards, then one should carefully consider whether it is true. Think about some of the stories you've been hearing in the news lately. Do you think they meet God's standards of truth?

PRAYER: Lord, it is such a relief that we can depend on you to be trustworthy. In an age where a lack of faithfulness and trust are becoming the norm, we can look to You. We can rely on you fully—the truthfulness of the words you speak, your loving motives, and your faithfulness in doing what you say. Thank you, Lord, for opening our eyes that we might know you. Help us to keep our eyes stayed on You. Amen.

Day 6

God is Trustworthy

> . . . The Lord is trustworthy in all he
> promises and faithful in all
> he does. —Psalm 145:13

There are many scriptures that point to the trustworthiness of God. This quality is understood as one who is "worthy of confidence", "able to be relied on to do or provide what is needed or right", and "deriving from a source worthy of belief".[3] God's trustworthiness and truthfulness go hand in hand.

The Bible teaches that all people will be judged by God and that his sentence on us will have eternal consequence. Since God will judge mankind, it is essential that his character be pure, just and trustworthy. Imagine what it would be like if the God who judged us was unclear on what was true or didn't have all the facts. How could his judgment be right? Fortunately, this is not the case. Because God is just and true, his judgments have been, are and will be righteous, fair and impartial. As it says in Deuteronomy 32:4, "He is the Rock, his works are perfect, and all his ways are just. A faithful God who does no wrong, upright and just is he."

Christian apologist Ravi Zacharias put it best when

he said, "The fact is, the truth matters – especially when you're on the receiving end of a lie. Nowhere is this more important than in the area of justice and judgment. After all, eternity is an awfully long time to be wrong."

Consider when you've been judged for something you did or said, or answers you gave on a test, or even a traffic violation. Did you want the judge to be fair and trustworthy?

PRAYER: Lord, you are a just and true God. We know that the day will come when we will all stand before you in judgment. You, Lord, whose name is Faithful and Just, will fairly and rightly review our lives, decisions and actions, and cast judgment on us. We pray that you will cover our sins with Jesus's blood and forgive us, Lord. We pray you will deliver us in that day and teach us compassion and mercy as we deal with others who have treated us wrongly. Amen.

Day 7

Foundation for Understanding

> . . . the Son of God has come and has given us understanding, so that we may know him who is true. And we are in him who is true by being in his Son Jesus Christ. He is the true God and eternal life. —1 John 5:20

As we grow closer to Jesus and deepen our relationship with Him, we increase in understanding and our ability to discern truth. Without this transformative power in our lives, we would remain in darkness. "For you were once darkness, but now you are light in the Lord. . ." (Ephesians 5:8).

Knowing that God is true is both comforting and a rare treasure. It is like the difference between a diamond and glass. Truth is valuable and rare. Whereas, deceit is commonplace and cheap. When truth is found, it shines and sparkles. Words of truthful men, like Abraham Lincoln or George Washington, are respected and immortalized. Lies however are easily discarded and forgotten.

Truth is the basis for understanding and expanding our knowledge and abilities. Paul teaches us that the root of knowledge is goodness and its full fruition is love. "For this very reason, make every effort to add to your faith goodness . . . knowledge . . . self-control . . . perseverance . . . godliness . . . mutual affection and . . . love" (2 Peter 1:5-7). As we remember that all of God's commands are summed up in love, we can see that godly character leads us to truth and truth leads us to love.

Daily we are bombarded with choices on what we hear and believe. How has knowing what is true increased your understanding? And when you deny truth, how does that hinder your understanding?

PRAYER: Lord, we thank you for your true character, your true word and your trustworthy actions toward us. In everything you do, say and think, Lord, you are defined by truth. Help us, Lord, to understand the truth found in your Word and to apply it to our lives. We ask that you will enable us to grow in understanding and wisdom as we draw near to You through prayer and your Word. Amen.

"He who permits himself to tell a lie once, finds it much easier to do it a second and third time, till at length it becomes habitual; he tells lies without attending to it, and truths without the world's believing him. This falsehood of the tongue leads to that of the heart, and in time depraves all its good dispositions." –Thomas Jefferson, letter to Peter Carr, August 19, 1785

II

How to Recognize Lies

God the Father, God the Son, the Word of God, and God's commands are trustworthy, true and everlasting. Deception and lying are contrary to God's true nature and incompatible with truth. God does not lie to or deceive mankind.

The Bible teaches that Satan is the "father of lies" (John 8:44). In *Thoughts Moral and Divine*, Wellins Calcott said "Lying is practiced to deceive, to injure, betray, rob, destroy, and the like; Lying in this sense is the concealing of all other crimes, the sheep's clothing upon the wolf's back, the Pharisee's prayer, the harlot's blush, the hypocrite's paint, and Judas's kiss . . . it is mankind's darling sin, and the Devil's distinguished characteristic."[4]

Christians are warned to avoid deceit and lies, since they are offensive to God. They are also instructed to be on guard and watchful for those who deceive and seek to harm them. In this next section, we will take a look at what the Bible reveals about the attributes of deceitful lying people.

Day 8

Lies are Deceptive

Watch out for false prophets. They come to
you in sheep's clothing, but inwardly they
are ferocious wolves. —Matthew 7:15

How do we recognize lies from truth? I read on the
internet that Mark Zuckerberg, the co-founder, CEO
and chairman of Facebook, had outlined 10 ways to
test Fake News in the media[5]. Three of Zuckerberg's
suggestions were to (1) Be skeptical of headlines, (2)
Investigate the source, and (3) Check the evidence.
From a worldly perspective, these are logical starting
points for testing the validity of a message. After all,
shouldn't we ensure that information is true before we
act on it or make decisions based on it?

When it impacts your life, economy, or political
interests, everyone should be interested in getting to
the truth. The Bible teaches that one way to test truth
is to look at the "fruit" (Matthew 7:16), or results and
actions of the messenger. First, a true messenger will
recognize God as the source of truth. Second, he will
exhibit righteous character consistent with truth. In
contrast, a false messenger will reject God. While they
may have the appearance of an innocent "sheep", they

will actually be "ferocious wolves" intent on harm (Matthew 7:15).

When we observe individuals, who don't take the time to validate information, we label them as ignorant and foolish. Proverbs 1:32 says, "For the waywardness of the simple will kill them, and the complacency of fools will destroy them." If we fail to test the truth around us, we become victims of the deceitful lying false message.

How do you test what you hear and read? What standard do you use to verify it is true?

PRAYER: Lord, thank you for your love and faithfulness to us. As a loving Father, you have carefully instructed us and warned us about the dangers around us. Help us, Lord, to have discerning hearts and to recognize the wolves in our lives and society. According to your Word, the angel of the Lord encamps around those who fear you and delivers them (Psalm 34:7). Protect us, Lord, and shield us from danger. Amen

Day 9

Lies are Destructive

> But there were also false prophets among
> the people, just as there will be false teachers
> among you. They will secretly introduce
> destructive heresies, even denying the
> sovereign Lord who bought them—bringing
> swift destruction on themselves. —2 Peter 2:1

Needing to differentiate truth from lies in society is nothing new. In New Testament times, people were faced with similar challenges. Yesterday, we looked at the importance of testing the validity of one's character and the source of information. In 2 Peter 2:1, the Bible shows us another way to test truth. A false message, or lie, will have a destructive effect.

Think about some of the news that has "leaked" without permission in recent months from sources that were thought to be secure. It is doubtful that the leaks were meant to build up those impacted by the disclosure, even if the sources felt justified in their actions. More often than not, the effect has been very destructive either intentionally or as a side-effect. Careers have been ruined and reputations tarnished. This is not how God works.

God tells us what we need to hear, the truth, so

that those who listen can be edified, blessed and grow nearer to him. Judgment falls on those who refuse to hear, not those who listen. In contrast, the intent of liars is to deceive and destroy. Psalm 52:2 says "You who practice deceit, your tongue plots destruction; it is like a sharpened razor."

When people have lied to you, even if it was well intended, how has it affected your life? Have you been built up or torn down? When you see lies in the news, do you think this has a negative or positive effect on your life, those around you and the nation?

PRAYER: Lord, you are a God who cares about our well-being. Your laws are good and edifying; they build us up. Unfortunately, we live in a world where Satan has domain. Satan is like a roaring lion seeking to devour mankind. His lies tear down the truth and men's lives. Help us, Lord, to stand firm in your Word, to fight lies and to build up the people in our lives with truth. Amen.

Day 10

Lies Lead to Bondage

> For they mouth empty, boastful words
> and, by appealing to the lustful desires
> of the flesh, they entice people who are
> just escaping from those who live in error.
> They promise them freedom, while they
> themselves are slaves of depravity—for
> "people are slaves to whatever has mastered
> them." —2 Peter 2:18-19

If you have read prophecies about the end times, one prominent individual during the final days before Jesus returns is the Antichrist. Not only is this individual a LIAR (in all caps), but he is characterized by his boastfulness (Daniel 7:8). He will deceive many and entice them away from godliness, even to the point of persecuting those who remain on the side of God.

Without realizing it, people who believe lies are enslaved and placed in bondage. They become "slaves to whatever has mastered them" (2 Peter 2:19). Unwittingly, they choose the path in which they will share the evil one's final outcome – death. Perhaps you have heard the metaphor of the boiling frog. The premise is that if a frog is put suddenly into boiling water, it will jump out, but if the frog is put in tepid water which is then brought to a boil slowly, it will not perceive the danger and will be cooked to death.

While there is some dispute as to whether scientifically this analogy is true, it does present a vivid picture as to what may happen if we tarry in a dangerous environment. That is how sin works. It gradually destroys our soul, as bit by bit sin deceives our hearts and the truth of the gospel is pushed out.

Today, become aware of those things around you that are de-sensitizing you to sin. Make a decision to reject evil and pursue God instead.

PRAYER: *Lord, we praise you and thank you for your deliverance. You son has died on the cross so that we can be delivered from the penalty of our sins and be reconciled to God. Yet we know that when we sin, we subject ourselves to the short-term consequence of our actions. Help us, Lord, to be obedient to your commands, so that we will not be enslaved by our sinful actions. Amen.*

Day 11

Lies Distort Truth

Many will follow their depraved conduct
and will bring the way of truth into
disrepute. —2 Peter 2:2

Not only do people tell willful lies, but evil people distort the truth to accomplish their goals. You've heard the common expression, "the end justifies the means." One well-known example was the trial of Jesus where the Jewish leaders condemned him to crucifixion even though he was innocent and had not committed any crime. Like many people today, they decided to distort the facts and willfully lie in order to accomplish their objective.

Distortions of the truth can be difficult to recognize. Pamela Meyer, author of *Liespotting: Proven Techniques to Detect Deception*, claims that we're lied to from 10 to 200 times per day.[6] On her blog site, she also recognized the difficulty in detecting lies, claiming that research shows that "humans detect lies with only 54% accuracy" and "between 75% and 82% of lies go undetected."[7]

There are many ways that people lie. In an article in The Huffington Post[8] five ways were highlighted–in controlling a response, lying by omission, exaggerations, self-protection, and gossip or covert conversation. Regardless of whether a lie is willful, the refusal to recognize the truth, or a modified replica of the truth, nothing good comes from lies. God hates lying so much that his response to this form ungodliness is "wrath" (Romans 1:18).

What should our response be? To protect ourselves, we must be on "guard" so that we are not inadvertently drawn into sin (Acts 20:30-31) by believing the lies. We should also test the accuracy of what we hear against the Word of God (1 John 4:1).

PRAYER: I am comforted, Lord, by your constant presence. As I walk through the day and am exposed to lies all about me, I seek a safe refuge and your gentle spirit of truth. It is the one place I can go and find protection and peace. Lord, surround me today with your presence and protect me from the flaming arrows of the evil one. Amen.

Day 12

Lies are Motivated by Greed

And in their greed they will exploit
you with false arguments and twisted
doctrine. . . —2 Peter 2:3 (AMP)

What motivates people to lie? According to 2 Peter 2:3, one motivation is greed. Greed is a close relative of coveting. While greed is the selfish and excessive desire for more of something than what is needed, coveting is the yearning to possess or have something that belongs to others. As individuals let greed and covetousness fester in their hearts, this ungodly desire soon takes an ugly form that can lead to a lack of fulfillment, deceit, threats and even theft to accomplish their ends.

One of the 10 commandments is "to not covet your neighbor's house, . . . wife, . . . servant, . . . ox or donkey, or anything that belongs to your neighbor" (Exodus 20:17). When we break this commandment, we fail to love our neighbor as ourselves. Greed is the result of a troubled unfulfilled heart. You may think that the only one affected by your greed is yourself. But greed, like coveting, has the extended effect of damaging relationships.

The sad truth about greed is that it is never satisfied. John D. Rockefeller once quipped, "If your only goal is to become rich, you will never achieve it."[9] There will always be something more to want. The solution is to learn to be "content in any and every situation, whether well fed or hungry, whether living in plenty or in want" (Philippians 4:12).

When we covet small things, we are tempted to discount the seriousness of our desire. However, if greed takes root in your heart, what do you think your future will hold for you? Consider those around you who might be hurt by this attitude.

PRAYER: Lord, you created every aspect of this world and beyond to the universe, even those things we haven't discovered yet. When we feel need or want, Lord, you can meet our needs abundantly. Teach us, Lord, to bring all our needs to you. Let us learn to pray and trust you for answers and to refuse to entertain greed and covetousness in our hearts. Amen.

Day 13

Lies Despise Authority

> This is especially true of those who follow
> the corrupt desire of the flesh and despise
> authority. . . these people blaspheme in matters
> they do not understand . . . —2 Peter 2:10a, 12

Another characteristic of a liar is a lack of respect for authority. As we read through 2 Peter 2, we see that in addition to being deceptive, destructive, enslaving, manipulating and greedy, false messengers are also unreasonable and reject authority (verse 10). Now that is some resume! It is a wonder that any of these folks find themselves in positions of influence, except they are so good at camouflaging their true character.

These individuals fail to understand the truth and its ramifications. Their judgment is clouded. As it says in verse 12, "they blaspheme [speak irreverently] about things they don't understand". And as their distorted passions and unfulfilled frustrations percolate in their darkened hearts, they become like unreasoning crazed animals. Surely if they realized their fates, they wouldn't willingly pursue this path.

As I watch the news on television, read the headlines on the internet, or scan the headlines in the magazines lining the check-out stand at the supermarket, it seems increasingly commonplace for individuals to reject authority and justify their unreasonable demands. As Christians, we must exercise discernment to avoid being swayed by their irreverence and lack of understanding.

How can you avoid the trap of becoming unreasonable? Keep a clear mind by refreshing your memory (2 Peter 1:13) in the truth of God's word.

PRAYER: Lord, I look up to you and stand in awe of your constancy and reasoning. You have created all things and understand their order and purpose. When men reject your truths, they lose sight of their purpose and your perfect plan. Help us, Lord, to not become like these unreasoning and disobedient men. Help us, Lord, to recognize your sovereignty in our lives and to submit willingly to your ways. Amen.

Day 14

A Life of Sinfulness

> But other people are selfish. They
> refuse to follow truth and, instead,
> follow evil. God will give them his
> punishment and anger. —Romans 2:8 (NCV)

Have you ever heard the expression, "The devil made me do it"? This expression highlights the things that people do that they know are wrong. Yet despite this they want to avoid any accountability or responsibility for their actions, so they blame the devil and feign an inability to control themselves.

Whether actions are out of control or purposeful, a man or woman's actions speak volumes about their heart condition. As the saying goes, "Actions speak louder than words."

Harmful sinful actions flow from a lying deceptive heart. In 2 Peter 2, we continue to see the traits of false messengers. These liars "carouse in broad daylight", "reveling in their pleasures" . . . and "they never stop sinning" (2 Peter 2:13-14). While we would like to trust what people say at face value, the scripture teaches us to also watch what people do. When it comes to evaluating truth, actions are the signposts.

A sinful lifestyle is detestable to God. More than

just being offended, the Bible teaches that God hates "haughty eyes, a lying tongue, hands that shed innocent blood, a heart that devises wicked schemes, feet that are quick to rush into evil, a false witness who pours out lies and a person who stirs up conflict in the community" (Proverbs 6:16-19).

Think about someone you know has lied to you or others. How have their actions betrayed their hearts? What do your actions say about you?

PRAYER: Lord, you are in heaven and your name is holy. Your kingdom will prevail once again on earth and your Son will come to judge mankind. Teach us your ways, Lord, that we may live forever in your presence. Forgive us when we sin. Lord, lead us not into temptation, but deliver us from evil. Amen.

Let us not love with words or speech...
but with actions & truth.
– C.S. Lewis

III

How to Recognize Truth

Liars are characterized as deceptive, destructive, enslaved by their behavior, distorting the truth, greedy, rebellious against authority, and indulging in a life of sin. When we see people acting this way we should be very cautious about believing what they say.

In contrast, God and all of his words and actions are characterized as being true. Children of God should be a reflection of their Father by speaking and living the truth. Our prayer should be "Show me your ways, Lord, teach me your paths. Guide me in your truth and teach me, for you are God my Savior, and my hope is in you all day long" (Psalm 25:4-5).

As we strive to discern what is true from that which is false, watching the behavior of individuals and listening to their words, we need to increase our discernment skills. In this next section let's look at scriptures which teach us the qualities that are consistent with people of truth.

Day 15

Truth Comes into the Light

> But whoever lives by the truth comes into
> the light, so that it may be seen plainly that
> what they have done has been done in the
> sight of God. —John 3:21

One important aspect of truth is that it can stand the test of light. When you put light on something, you can see the details. Nothing is hidden. If a person's actions or words cannot withstand the scrutiny of inspection and has to remain in the shadows, that is a certain indication that it may be false.

The Greek word for "truth" is *aletheia*, which literally means to "un-hide" or "hiding nothing." It conveys the thought that truth is always there, always open and available for all to see, with nothing being hidden or obscured. When our lives are based on truth, we don't have to hide anything from those around us. We won't need cover-up stories to camouflage our deeds or character. We can be honest and forthright.

Not only can truth stand the test of light, it also provides guidance to us. "Your [true] word is a lamp for my feet, a light on my path." (Psalm 119:105). And we should "walk in the light, as he is in the light" (1 John 1:7). Imagine if you were camping in the woods. As the sun goes down and darkness envelops the campground, you would need a flashlight beaming down on the pathway to avoid stumbling. Likewise, truth keeps us from falling

As you listen to or read the news each day, analyze it carefully like a detective. When the news story is challenged, do the sources duck behind excuses or fail to give a direct answer? Are they unwilling to provide evidence? If so, perhaps the story is unable to stand the test of light.

PRAYER: The Lord is God and he has made his light shine on us (Psalm 118:27). How precious is your light, Lord. It reveals your ways and guides us on the path to righteousness. Help us this day to live a life that withstands the revealing nature of light. Help us to be a light to those around us, showing them the path to your Son. Amen.

~≈∽•─────────────────────────────────

Truth Reveals Itself as Genuine

> You may say to yourselves, "How can we
> know when a message has not been spoken
> by the LORD?" If what a prophet proclaims
> in the name of the LORD does not take place
> or come true, that is a message the LORD has
> not spoken. —Deuteronomy 18:21-22

The enduring quality of an item, a person or a friendship is confirmed as genuine if it "will stand the test of time." We are all too familiar with the reality that people tell lies. However, even if we are unsuccessful in uncovering lies in the short term, we are confident that over time they will be found out. As individuals who conceal them die or new revelations come to light, truth has a way of being ultimately revealed.

In the early days of Israel, there were many prophets who claimed to have a message from God. How could God's people discern truth from fiction? According to Deuteronomy 18:22, there was a simple test – TIME. During the lifetime of a prophet he would make both short-term and long-term prophecies. The short-term prophecies were necessary to validate a prophet. If any of the short-term prophecies did not come to pass exactly to the detail foreseen, then the individual was exposed as a false prophet. A true prophet of God would be proven in the fulfillment of their prophecies.

We see this today as well. There are modern day predictors of the future, such as Nostradamus, who claim to have all the answers. Our challenge is to pay attention and be discerning as to the genuineness of these individuals. Don't be too hasty to rush after their predictions, but rather take the time to validate their authenticity.

PRAYER: Lord, you are the Alpha and Omega, the beginning and the end, eternal and unchanging. Your Word has withstood the test of time and proven itself to be trustworthy and constant. Help us, Lord, to be wise, to seek truth and to live according to its precepts. Help us to be genuine and real, committed to the truth. Amen.

Day 17

Truth does not Harm a Neighbor

> LORD, who may dwell in your sacred
> tent? Who may live on your holy mountain?
> The one whose walk is blameless, who does
> what is righteous, who speaks the truth
> from their heart . . . Whoever does these
> things will never be shaken.
> —Psalm 15:1-2, 5

Have you ever heard of the harmless white lie? This common expression refers to those lies that we tell that are minor, diplomatic or a well-intentioned untruth. But is there such a thing? Are there lies that are okay to tell? Or are all lies harmful?

If we use the character of an individual who wants to approach God as a filter, the answer is that all lies are harmful. Psalm 15:2 teaches us that an individual must speak truth from his heart and be blameless to dwell in God's tent. In Psalm 15:3, the various types of falsehoods are listed – slander, doing wrong to a neighbor, and casting a slur. These actions are considered evil by God because lies harm others.

In contrast, in Psalm 15:4-5 we see that a truthful man will despise a vile person, honor those who fear God, keep an oath even when it hurts, lend money to the poor and not accept a bribe against the innocent. Not only does truth not harm a neighbor, it actually helps them, can be trusted and stands up for their well-being.

When I think about all the white lies that are told with the best intention, I am convicted by God's high standard of righteous truth. White lies start small, but they begin to whittle away at our conscience allowing bigger lies to take root. Our tongues have the potential to do harm or to do good. Consider today the steps needed to tame your tongue. Redirect your speech to tell the truth and build up others.

PRAYER: Lord, it is impossible for you to lie. When you speak, we can be assured that you will act. When God promises something, we can be sure that He will fulfill it. (Numbers 23:19). Lord, we trust the promises in your Word, because we know you are a God of truth. Teach us to walk in truth and do no harm to our neighbors. Help us be individuals that those around us can rely on. Amen.

Day 18

Truth is a Stabilizing Force

And ye shall know the truth, and the truth
shall make you free. —John 8:32 (KJV)

Freedom. Liberty. Justice. As Americans, we are all familiar with the ring of these remarkable words in our Pledge of Allegiance. Yet have you considered the importance that the truth has on these concepts? Freedom, liberty and justice cannot exist in the midst of anarchy and lies. If we can't rely on our leaders to be truthful, or for the laws of our nation to be based on truth and to exist for the well-being of our people, or for courts to be just, then we are in a downward spiral as a nation and at risk of losing these privileges.

Many colleges use an excerpt from John 8:32 as their motto— "the truth shall make you free." But quoting just these few words is not reflective of the complete teaching of Jesus. When Jesus spoke these words, he was speaking about something much higher than book learning. He was speaking about truth that is derived from obeying God. He said, "[31] . . . If you hold to my teaching, you are really my disciples. [32] Then you will know the truth, and the truth will set you free" (John 8:31-32). When we reduce truth to worldly knowledge alone, apart from living a godly life, it is like knocking the legs out from it. Truth will not be able to perform at its full potential.

Our nation's founders also understood the importance of truth that is founded in the teachings of the scriptures. For this reason, the official motto of the United States is "In God we Trust". My prayer today is that as a nation we will repent of our sins and return to seeking truth that is found in following the one true God. I ask you to join me in that prayer.

PRAYER: Father, forgive us for our sins as a nation. We know that you are a God who loves truth and righteousness. We know that we cannot find truth in our own power; truth can only be found with You at its source. Help us, Father, to not stand idly by as our nation rejects the truth. Help us to do all in our power to stand firm for those principles that are found in your Word. Amen.

Day 19

Truth Brings Healing

The words of the reckless pierce
like swords, but the tongue of the wise
brings healing. —Proverbs 12:18

Our words have a big impact on those around us. We can speak truth or we can speak lies. Our words can build up or tear down. Our words can lead people to Christ or they can deceive them to follow Satan's lies.

One influence that we often overlook is the ability for our words to heal people. "Gracious words are a honeycomb, sweet to the soul and healing to the bones" (Psalm 16:24).

Consider a neighbor who has just lost a spouse. Coming beside them with an arm around the shoulder and kind words bring them comfort. Or consider a friend who is going through a destructive divorce. Words of wisdom can help them through tough days, faltering self-confidence, and guilt as they are encouraged to seek God and do what is right for their home. Or consider someone who is dying or very ill. Loving and compassionate words have the power to give them added strength to endure their suffering.

God's truth has the same impact on us. Whether we are physically ill, emotionally broken or spiritually lost,

God is able to restore us. In Exodus 15:26, God's name is Jehovah Rapha, the God who heals us. We are healed when we listen to God, do what is right in his eyes, pay attention to his commands, and keep his decrees. In other words, truth and righteousness are healing.

Wouldn't you like to be an individual who brings comfort and healing to those around you? Consider today how you can speak healing into someone's life.

PRAYER: Lord, you are Jehovah Rapha, the great Healer. You are able Lord to take our broken spirits and broken bodies and make them whole again. You have allowed us to be conduits of your healing through kind, compassionate, loving, sincere and true words and actions. Help our words, Lord, to be soothing and comforting to those around us. Amen.

Day 20

Truth Brings Joy

Light shines on the righteous and joy on the
upright in heart. —Psalm 97:11

When I was a young girl, I remember a song by
Johnny Lee, called "Looking for Love". One of the
verses bemoaned the futility of his search as "looking
for love in all the wrong places". I often feel this
describes our search for joy. We seek joy in a variety
of ways—through increased possessions, escape from
responsibilities, a weekend repose with nature, and a
host of other pursuits. But how often do we find it?

According to the Oxford Dictionary, joy is a feeling
of great pleasure and happiness[10]. It's that feeling we get
when all is right in the world, as our gloomy spirits and
concerns of the day melt away.

For all our attempts to find joy in our own efforts,
the Bible teaches that it is actually a gift from the true
God. John 15:9-11 points to the root of joy – walking
in God's love and keeping his commandments. This
explains why godly joy is so often accompanied by
the peace and the assurance of a life centered in God.
When truth and righteousness abound, peace and joy
are the results. Proverbs 12:20 states simply "those who
promote peace have joy."

In contrast, there exists a worldly joy that tends to be short-lived. It is a joy based on our circumstance and actions. Since the conditions of the world are tenuous at best and, unfortunately, we are surrounded by people who are often unreliable and have flawed character, this joy usually does not last.

How can we be filled with a joy that lasts? Resolve today to be men and women who promote peace (Proverbs 12:20) and seek God's kingdom and his righteousness (Matthew 6:33).

PRAYER: The joy of the Lord is my strength (Nehemiah 8:10). As I ponder these words in my mind, I am reminded of what a loving and good God you are. That you have brought joy into my heart and lifted me up from my despair. I praise you, Lord, for the perfect joy that you place in the hearts of those who love you. Amen.

Day 21

Truth Endures Forever

> Truthful lips endure forever, but a lying
> tongue lasts only a moment. —Proverbs 12:19

It is hard to imagine anything spoken will last forever. There are a few men and women who have inspired generations that are still quoted today. But imagine our words having such a deep impact on the people around us that they actually endure forever. Or that are words are so worthless that they only last a moment and then are forgotten.

We have been taught that God existed before creation and will be here long after our short span on this earth. God is eternal, the Alpha and Omega, the beginning and end. What God knew and understood from the beginning, the truth about creation and righteousness, remains. Just as God is immutable, that is he never changes, truth is always truth. Truth doesn't change nor is it redefined with each popular movement or most recent fad and outlook. Real truth is constant and it endures forever.

Mary Todd Lincoln, the wife of Abraham Lincoln, once said "Clouds and darkness surround us, yet Heaven is just, and the day of triumph will surely come, when justice and truth will be vindicated." This insightful comment was spoken with a confidence that could only be grounded in the knowledge that truth was steadfast, dependable, and in the end, knowable. To judge others based on a lie would be unjust. It is only in the presence of an eternal truth that we can we find true justice.

This is the kind of truth I want. A truth I can depend on. A truth that doesn't change. A truth that endures. Today, seek to find real truth and begin to make it a part of your life.

PRAYER: You are a constant God, never changing and always abiding in truth. We can depend on you absolutely. Since the beginning of time and for eternity, your truth will stand. Change me, Lord, into someone who loves you completely with my mind, body and spirit. Help me to seek a truth that endures forever. Amen.

Renewing the mind is a little like refinishing furniture. It is a two-stage process. It involves taking off the old and replacing it with the new. The old is the lies you have learned to tell or were taught by those around you; it is the attitudes and ideas that have become a part of your thinking but do not reflect reality. The new is the truth. To renew your mind is to involve yourself in the process of allowing God to bring to the surface the lies you have mistakenly accepted and replace them with truth. To the degree that you do this, your behaviour will be transformed.
– Charles Stanley, Pastor

IV

Become Agents of Truth

In our devotions, we have reviewed the pure, unvarnished and desirable characteristics of truth. But this raises a question—is it enough to know the truth? What is knowledge without action?

One of my favorite verses is found in Jeremiah 29:12-13. "Then you will call on me and come and pray to me, and I will listen to you. You will seek me and find me when you seek me with all your heart." It is a wonderful assurance that we can find God and that he will listen to his children. But when we read it closely, God's listening is predicated on our calling on God, coming to him, and praying. And finding God is predicated on us seeking with intentional effort, "with all [our] heart".

Becoming someone who represents and speaks truth is not easy. It will require effort and an honest pursuit of truth. And once truth is found, it will take practice and development of skills. Let us now consider how we can become agents of truth.

Day 22

Study God's Word

> Study and do your best to present yourself to
> God approved, a workman [tested by trial]
> who has no reason to be ashamed, accurately
> handling and skillfully teaching the word of
> truth. —2 Timothy 2:15 (AMP)

I read once that federal agents who are trained to catch counterfeiters spend a lot of time handling, looking at and studying real money. The idea is that the more familiar you are with the real thing, the easier it will be to identify that which is fake.

In scriptures, we are taught that the best way to handle and teach the truth, is that 5-letter word that most of us hate – STUDY. In 2 Timothy 3:16-17, Paul confirms that the Word of God is for the express purpose of "teaching, rebuking, correcting, and training" in righteousness.

To study and apply God's word, there are five easy steps. First, faith comes from "hearing . . . the word about Christ (Romans 10:17). Second, we should read God's word (Deuteronomy 17:19) for ourselves. Third, we should study and examine scriptures regularly to test our understanding (Acts 17:11). Fourth, memorizing scriptures etches them on the tablet of our hearts

(Proverbs 7:3), thus making it easier to form habits. Fifth, meditate on (Psalm 1:2) and consider the truths, their effect on lives around you and ways to apply them (James 1:22).

Part of recognizing lies and falsehoods, or as our contemporary media puts it – fake news, is to become familiar with truth. As we know truth and it becomes second nature to us, then the contrast of lies and deception will suddenly become clear. Do you feel prepared to recognize deception in this world? Resolve today to become better equipped in this area.

PRAYER: Lord, your Word is right and true. We know that it is right for us to study and meditate on your word. Help us, Lord, to do our best to become individuals who accurately handle and teach the truth. We pray that your Spirit will transform us and give us the strength we need to do what is right in your sight. Amen.

Day 23

Think About Truth

> Finally, brothers and sisters, whatever
> is true, whatever is noble, whatever is
> right, whatever is pure, whatever is lovely,
> whatever is admirable—if anything is
> excellent or praiseworthy—think about
> such things. —Philippians 4:8

In Philippians 4:8, we are exhorted to think about things that are noble, lovely and admirable. Perhaps we've seen this—a brave soldier, or an individual who takes a courageous stand for another's rights, or a beautiful sunrise, or a clear mountain brook trickling through the forest nourishing life with its pristine waters. Such thoughts give us pleasure, replenish our souls and inspire us.

We are also encouraged to think about that which is true, right and pure. These may be more difficult to find. Yet when we find them, we should cherish them and reflect on them often. Perhaps we've seen them in the inspired words of an orator, or in unselfish acts of compassion and mercy, or even in the innocence of a child.

In thinking about these things, we are not talking about a shallow, acknowledgement of their existence.

But rather, we are talking about a deep consideration of and meditation on truth, just like a cow chews a cud. We need to chew, chew, chew, until we extract every ounce of enlightenment.

Proverbs 23:7 teaches that a person becomes and is a reflection of what he "thinks in his heart". As we meditate on truth, we are literally transforming our character. Truth begins to fill a larger part of our being as deception and lies are pushed out.

Make it the goal of each day to think on these things. Then start chewing on and unraveling truth's mysteries by asking questions -- Why is it true? How does knowing this make the world better? How can we use this to bless others?

PRAYER: Father, you are Elohim, God "Creator, Mighty and Strong" (Genesis 1:1). There is nothing impossible for you. Lord, teach me to consider your mighty and true ways, that I might worship you in truth. Amen.

Day 24

Discern the Truth

Who is wise? Let them realize these things.
Who is discerning? Let them understand.
The ways of the LORD are right; the
righteous walk in them, but the rebellious
stumble in them. —Hosea 14:9

According to Webster, discernment is "the quality of being able to grasp and comprehend what is obscure; an act of perceiving something; a power to see what is not evident to the average mind."[11] Individuals who have this ability will be able to spot underlying motives and attitudes, sniff out hypocrites, and distinguish truth from lies.

Discernment and understanding go hand in hand. In Hosea 14:9, understanding and obedience to God's ways are characteristic of the discerning individual. Furthermore, true discernment comes from God. "The person without the Spirit does not accept the things that come from the Spirit of God but considers them foolishness, and cannot understand them because they are discerned only through the Spirit" (1 Corinthians 2:14).

To grow in discernment, we look to Hebrews 5:14. "But solid food is for the mature, who by constant use have trained themselves to distinguish good from evil." First, we should become firmly rooted in our understanding of God's word, "solid food". Second, we must apply God's word to our lives and obey it. And finally, we "train ourselves" to distinguish good and evil, by persistent application, practice, and testing what we see and hear (1 Thessalonians 5:20-22).

As we become more established in the knowledge of truth, its source and its characteristics, our ability to discern truth from lies increases.

PRAYER: Lord, how can we know truth apart from you? It is impossible to find a pearl, if we don't look inside an oyster. Likewise, it is impossible to find truth, if we don't seek the source which is You. I pray that you will give us discernment, Lord, and that we will find understanding as we grow closer to You (Psalm 119:125). Amen

Day 25

Seek Wisdom

If any of you lacks wisdom, you should
ask God, who gives generously to all
without finding fault, and it will be
given to you. — James 1:5

Discernment is the ability to know whether motives or attitudes are genuine. Wisdom goes one step further. In addition to discerning intent, wisdom is the ability to accurately apply God-given insights to life. When it comes to truth, it is important that we not just know about it or recognize it, but that we also wisely apply truth to every area of our lives.

When it is time to select a Supreme Court Justice, a lot of discussion ensues as the President and Senate interview a candidate. There are days of questioning as leaders of the country try to discern the motives of the prospective candidate and how he or she would act out their viewpoints as they sit in judgment of cases having national importance. They understand that what really matters is how this individual's thinking will impact their actions.

True wisdom comes from God alone. In Proverbs 9:10, it says that the "fear of the Lord is the beginning of wisdom, and knowledge of the Holy

One is understanding." Secondly, godly wisdom is characterized by peace, consideration, submission to God, mercy, justice and truth (James 3:17). There is very little objection to a person who exhibits these qualities in his life.

The Bible teaches that "those who are wise will shine like the brightness of the heavens, and those who lead many to righteousness, like the stars for ever and ever" (Daniel 12:3). Today, seek to be wise in the discernment and application of the truth. Add action and good works to your knowledge of the truth, wisely discerning how to live out what the scriptures teach you.

PRAYER: Lord, help us to go beyond knowing the truth. Help us to apply truth wisely to our day-to-day activities and long-term plans. We pray that You will enable us to shine in wisdom like the stars of heaven for ever and ever. Amen.

Day 26

Wear the Belt of Truth

Stand firm then, with the belt of truth buckled
around your waist, with the breastplate of
righteousness in place, and with your feet
fitted with the readiness that comes from the
gospel of peace. —Ephesians 6:14-15

In Ephesians 6:14-15 we look at the spiritual clothing of a righteous man. In the time of the apostles, Roman guards were seen all around the community and were clothed for war. They wore a belt around their waist, a breastplate to shield them from arrows, and footwear ready for long journeys.

The belt worn around the waist of a Roman soldier was not a simple leather strap such as we wear today. It was a thick, heavy leather and metal band with a protective piece hanging down in front of it. The belt held the soldier's sword and other weapons. It was important for not only securing their outer garb, but ensuring they could move swiftly and without impediment, armed and ready for battle as they fought off enemies and protected their territories.

It was this image that was brought to mind, when Paul exhorted believers to stand firm with the belt of truth about their waist. Truth should secure our understanding and prepare us for battle both defensively and offensively as we encounter threats in life. This belt of truth symbolically holds the sword of the Spirit, linking truth and the Word of God (John 17:17).

As you dress for work today, consider whether you are dressed both physically and spiritually for the day that lies ahead for you. A short devotion in the morning before work is a great way to prepare your heart and mind for the day.

PRAYER: Lord, we stand before you as your humble servants. We acknowledge that you are the one true God and it is right that we submit our ways to you. As we prepare our hearts and minds for the day, teach us to prepare for the day spiritually. Clothe us, Lord, with truth, righteousness and the gospel of peace. Amen.

Day 27

Live as Children of Light

> For you were once darkness, but now you are
> light in the Lord. Live as children of light (for
> the fruit of the light consists in all goodness,
> righteousness and truth) and find out what
> pleases the Lord. —Ephesians 5:8-10

Light is a wonderful creation. There are many sources of light in nature – the sun, the moon, and the stars. Even in the creatures around us, we occasionally find those that have chemicals in their bodies that can be turned on to illuminate their way. It is easier to see your surroundings with more light. With less light, shadows and darkness obscure objects. It is not difficult to conclude that light is better than darkness when it comes to seeing things.

So, how do we live as children light? In Ephesians 5:8-10, we learn that the fruit of light is goodness, righteousness and truth, all of which please God. Goodness refers to one's virtue as evidenced by their benevolence and good works. Righteousness refers to one's moral state, seeking and obeying God. Truth is the pure and just outpouring of word and deed, coming from a godly heart.

When we live in truth, we have nothing to hide.

That is why we are described as light, as opposed to darkness. "You are the light of the world" (Matthew 5:14).

Today, consider how you can live in truth in every aspect of your life. Refuse to support lies. This doesn't mean that you have to reveal everything you know, particularly if the information is sensitive or confidential. But avoid being deceptive. Be a man or woman that walks in the light.

PRAYER: Lord, you are the everlasting light and glory of Zion (Isaiah 60:19). Not only are You light, but you are able to overcome our darkness and transform it into light (Psalm 18:28). Thank you, Lord, for all that you do in our lives. Transform us, Lord, and wash us clean from our sins. There is no place too deep for you to reach us. There is no place too far away that you can't find us. Praise be to God who is able to save us. Amen.

Day 28

Speak Truth

> . . . "Speak the truth to each other, and render
> true and sound judgment in your courts; do
> not plot evil against each other, and do not
> love to swear falsely. I hate all this," declares
> the LORD. —Zechariah 8:16-17

As children of God, we are to live and speak the truth.
This is the ultimate expression of freedom and liberty.
Imagine never having to hide an untruth or regret a
deception! We are free to be transparent because we
have the knowledge that we speak the truth and our
lives are characterized by truth.

The apostle John encouraged fellow Christians
to "not love with words or speech" alone, a shallow
expression of intent. But instead, we should love "with
actions and in truth" (1 John 3:18), the culmination
and proof of God living in us. This takes our words
to a higher level, a level of accountability and social
responsibility.

In contrast, God hates it when we plot evil against
each other, tell lies, or make commitments (oaths) that
we do not intend to keep. Just as God treats each of his
children with love, truth, respect and justice, He asks
that we treat each other the same way.

It is a privilege and responsibility to handle truth correctly. Albert Einstein quipped "Whoever is careless with the truth in small matters cannot be trusted with important matters." Our handling of truth shows others that we can be trusted confidents as they open up and share their hearts with us.

Resolve today to speak truth in love. Let your actions be loving, gentle, kind and truthful. You may be surprised how people around you respond as they discover they can rely on you to be trustworthy.

PRAYER: Lord, you are the true God. All your words are true. Teach us today to speak the truth, that others may know we are your children. Tame our words, Lord, and give them the power to do good. Give us courage as we share the good news of the gospel with those who are lost. We commit our words to you this day that they may be used for your glory. Amen.

Standing courageously for an unpopular opinion isn't easy, but the rewards of standing courageously for the truth will last forever. – Rick Warren

V

Truth Characterizes Children of God

God is the source of truth. He has revealed the characteristics of truth and lies in His word, enabling us to be discerning and wise. As God's truth dwells in us, we are transformed into individuals who speak and live truthfully.

Being truthful is more than doing the right thing. In becoming agents of truth, we show the world that we are sincere and authentic children belonging to and loving God.

Each time we compromise the truth, we give Satan a foothold to discredit both us and the God we serve. How can something so valuable, genuine truth, be treated with so casual an attitude.

Let us consider how we can live holy and godly lives (2 Peter 3:11), committed to truth and righteousness. Pray that God will empower you to live in a way that pleases him. For "he who began a good work in you will carry it on to completion until the day of Christ Jesus" (Philippians 1:6).

Day 29

Worship in Spirit and Truth

> Yet a time is coming and has now come when
> the true worshipers will worship the Father in
> the Spirit and in truth, for they are the kind of
> worshipers the Father seeks. — John 4:23

Ask yourself, what standard do I measure truth by? Do I measure truth by some internal barometer in myself? Or is it based on my current understanding, the latest article on the internet or the paper, or what someone is articulating in the news that sounds reasonable? Can my perception of truth be swayed?

If your answer to these questions is yes, then you stand with the majority of people in this world. But the danger with this point of view is that cultural truth is subject to change. And if truth is subject to change, is it really true?

The Hebrew word for truth is *emeth*, which implies firmness, constancy and durability. This is the truth of the scriptures, a constant truth, and only God's Spirit can reveal it (John 16:13) to people.

Part of worshipping God is seeking and understanding truth. But it also about loving God honestly and sincerely, as evidenced by obedience. Jesus said "Anyone who loves me will obey my teaching"

(John 14:23). Obedience forms a reciprocal bond of love and fellowship between God and man.

As we worship God, we will remember his deeds and miracles, consider all his works and mediate on his mighty deeds, for He is holy and deserving (Psalm 77:11-13) In reverence, we will humble ourselves before God.

Charles Stanley once said, "We are either in the process of resisting God's truth or in the process of being shaped and molded by his truth." Which one are you?

PRAYER: You are a God who is holy, deserving of worship, deserving of obedience, the rightful heir and creator of all that we see and don't see. My mind can scarcely understand how immensely holy and deserving You are. Lord, help me to worship you in spirit and truth. Help me to worship you as you rightly deserve. Amen.

Day 30

Draw Near to God

The LORD is near to all who call on him, to all
who call on him in truth. —Psalm 145:18

Did you know that God is discerning? He looks at
mankind, their heart and actions, and discerns whether
they are characterized by truth or lies. For those
individuals who are defined by truth, they have the
immense honor of being close to God, for God is near
"to all who call on him in truth" (Psalm 145:18).

Imagine the difference between someone who is near
to God versus one who is distant from God. When you
are physically close to a person, you can see the details
of their face – the color of their eyes, the wrinkles on
their forehead, the mole on their cheek. You can almost
smell their breath as they talk to you (sometimes not
a good thing). You can feel the heat from their body.
There is a closeness that is tangible. Well, being near
to God is just as personal. You begin to see the detail
characteristics of God. You feel his presence and notice
those things which make him unique and special.

In contrast, when you are far from God it is
difficult to know him well. There is no comfort from
his presence or words. His habits are strange to you. His
features are easily forgotten.

God desires for us to draw near to Him. In James 4:8, it says "Come near to God and he will come near to you." Today, let us draw near to our Lord in truth through honest prayer, genuinely seeking his word, and cleansing impure thoughts from our mind.

PRAYER: Lord, you have demonstrated your perfect love to us in that your son has died for our sins while we were undeserving and still sinners (Romans 5:8). That is amazing love! Guide us as we seek you with all our heart. Teach us through your Holy Spirit and place your plans and desires in our heart. Show us how to draw near to you in truth, so that we can abide in your presence for eternity and have a personal relationship with you. Amen.

Day 31

Be Sons of God

> And I will ask the Father, and he will give
> you another advocate to help you and be
> with you forever— the Spirit of truth . . .
> you know him, for he lives with you and
> will be in you. —John 14:16-17

As we come to the end of our devotion on truth, we have seen that God is the essence of truth. Every aspect of God is true and trustworthy, including God's son, his Holy Spirit and his Word.

Everything that is God and comes from God reflects the nature of God's character, including those who worship and obey God in truth. "This is how we know that we belong to the truth and how we set our hearts at rest in his presence . . . The one who keeps God's commands lives in him, and he in them" (1 John 3:19, 24).

As children of God, cleansed by the blood of Christ and empowered by the Holy Spirit, we become agents of truth. As we live and worship in truth, we prove our salvation and that we are heirs of God (Romans 8:17).

As the Holy Spirit works in us, transforming us from slaves bound by sin into children clothed in righteousness, we morph into men and women who honor God. We study God's word. We dwell on truth. We discern truth. We seek wisdom so that we can apply the truth to our actions. We live in truth. We speak truth. We live holy godly lives.

This is a big order for any of us to fill in our own strength. But with the help and support of God's Holy Spirit, we are equipped so that we can live grounded in truth and avoid deception.

God loves us deeply. His truth has bathed us in righteousness, giving us hope. May God bless you and keep you as you walk each day in truth.

PRAYER: Lord, you are our strength and power. In You, all things are possible. Fill us, Lord, with your Holy Spirit, enabling us to know the truth, to live in the truth, and to speak the truth. Thank you for sending your son, Jesus, that we might find hope and become children of God. Amen.

About the Author

DeLinda N. Baker is the author of <u>The Messiah's Imminent Return: Are You Ready?</u>.

She attended the University of Texas at Austin, majored in accounting and graduated in 1977 with a bachelor's degree in business.

Professionally, DeLinda started out in accounting and then became a technical consultant assisting companies in moving manual accounting processes onto computerized systems. For the remainder and bulk of her career, she was a project manager for technical, process, and merger initiatives for a major national bank. In this capacity, she moved up in rank until she retired in 2015.

While she was raised in a Christian family, it was toward the end of her sophomore year in college that DeLinda felt the tug of the Holy Spirit and made a commitment to follow and live for Jesus. From that day on, her life began to change as God began to work in her life.

DeLinda began to discover different gifts and desires. Early in her walk with the Lord, among those gifts, she found she had a deep desire to teach. While initially she led Bible studies developed by other authors, she later began to develop her own studies on topics that plagued Christians and were often misrepresented in our culture. Her passion in teaching is to be true to the Word of God and to not add or subtract from the teachings of scripture.

DeLinda has served as deacon in her church for several years, actively participated in the leadership of the women's ministry, led Sunday school classes, and assisted with administrative and financial projects in the church.

She is married to her husband of over 35 years, Robert, and has three adult children.

Endnotes

1   Online Merriam Webster dictionary, "Truth"; https://www. merriam-webster.com/dictionary/truth

2   Proclamation 3560—Thanksgiving Day, November 5, 1963, John F. Kennedy, President of the United States, 1961-1963

3   Online Merriam Webster dictionary, "Trustworthy"; https:// www.merriam-webster.com/dictionary/trustworthy

4   Wellins Calcott, *Thoughts Moral and Divine*, originally issued in London in 1756; second edition at Birmingham in 1758; third edition at Coventry in 1759; fourth edition at Manchester in 1761; and fifth edition at Exeter in 1764

5   Technodrine, "Facebook publishes 10 tips to discover "false news"", 8/15/2017, http://technodrime.com/2017/08/15/ facebook-publishes-10-tips-discover-false-news/

6   Pamela Meyers, TED talk "How to Spot a Liar", https:// www.ted.com/talks/pamela_meyer_how_to_spot_a_liar

7   Pamela Meyers, *LieSpotting: Proven Techniques to Detect Deception*, Blog "10 Research Findings to Detect Deception that will Blow your Mind"; http://liespotting.com/2010/06/ 10-research-findings-about-deception-that-will-blow-your-mind/

8   http://www.huffingtonpost.com/lisa-firestone/telling-the-truth_b_3831304.html).

9   John D. Rockefeller, *Complete Speaker's and Toastmaster's Library* (1992) edited by Jacob Morton Braude and Glenn Van Ekeren

10 Online Oxford dictionary, "Joy"; https://en.oxforddictionaries. com/definition/joy

11 Online Merriam Webster dictionary, "Discernment"; https:// www.merriam-webster.com/dictionary/discernment

Printed in the United States
By Bookmasters